UJU ORAMAH

ABC† of MAKING HEAVEN

A Blueprint for Earthly Success and Eternal Life

ABC of Making Heaven

Uju Oramah

ABC of Making Heaven

A Blueprint for Earthly Success and Eternal Life

DEDICATION

To my beloved father, Virgilius Azubuike,

For blessing me with life's greatest treasure: the knowledge of God.

ABC of Making Heaven
A Blueprint for Earthly Success & Eternal Life
DivineChild Publishers, Antioch, Tennessee.
Copyright © 2025
ISBN: 978-1-966820-00-0
Library of Congress Control Number: 2025900595
For Donations, bulk purchases, copies & other great titles, **please visit ujuoramah.com. Or**
email: divinechildpublishers@gmail.com

Also, get Copies at
Amazon
divinechildpublishers.com
ujuoramah.com

ABC of Making Heaven

This Book Belongs to

....

Your voices give us existence. Please support us by providing an honest review on Amazon. To share your feedback, scan this QR code or search for Uju Oramah on Amazon. Thank you for your assistance!

Get your free workbook for ABC of Making Heaven here
ujuoramah.com

Note: For additional Faith resources and free downloads, subscribe to ujuoramah.com
&
Check out the following YouTube channel for free Resources.

Virgin Mary & Catholic Faith
Uju Oramah: Think Faith Think Victory

Uju Oramah

Table of Contents

DEDICATION i
This Book Belongs to ii
PREFACE.. 3
Author's Note 5
Introduction 7
Why This Book?... 7
The Importance of an Eternal Perspective................... 8
Chapter 1 9
Knowledge of God: The Foundation of Everything........... 9
CHAPTER 2... 12
Knowledge of Self: Understanding Our Nature
and Need for Grace 12
Chapter 3 16
Embracing Humility: The Gateway to God's Grace 16
Chapter 4 22
What God Loves: Living a Life That Pleases Him 22
Chapter 5 26
God's Dislikes: What Offends God and What
He Calls Us to Avoid 26
Chapter 6 32

Repentance and Forgiveness: Pathways to Healing and Renewal 32

The Transformative Power of Repentance and Forgiveness 33

Chapter 7 37

Tribulations: The Refining Process Toward Holiness 37

Chapter 8 42

Self-Deliverance and Spiritual Warfare – Walking in the Light of Christ 42

Chapter 9 49

Pray Without Ceasing: Your Lifeline to God 49

Chapter 10 53

The Power of the Holy Spirit in Our Lives: Bearing Fruit . 53

Chapter 11 58

Live in Intimacy with God: Encountering God Through Personal Experience 58

Moving from Knowledge About God to Truly Knowing Him 58

Final Words: Living for Eternity, A Life Well-Lived for God 62

PREFACE

One of the reasons why God created us is to live forever with him in heaven. The petty catechism gave the reasons why God created us to include the following: to know him, to love him, to serve him, and to live forever with him in eternity. This is because God made us in his own image and likeness (Gen. 1:26). God made us and we belong to him. We are the sheep of his pasture (Ps.100: 3). Heaven is therefore the natural goal of every human being. The human being naturally desires happiness. Human beings desire to be at the place where eye has not seen, nor the ear heard, nor has it entered the mind of man, the things God prepared for those who love him (1 Cor. 2: 9). Human beings desire the presence of God. Human beings desire to see God as he really is (1 Jn. 3:2) Heaven is the sum total of all happiness because heaven is the presence of God.

The thoughts of heaven inspired the author to write this wonderful book entitled 'The ABC of Making Heaven'. Notwithstanding the fact that there is no easy way to go to heaven because the journey to heaven takes us through the narrow way (Matt. 7: 13-14), the writer made laudable efforts to convey some helpful ways to the journey towards the kingdom of heaven. She addressed many areas of the spiritual life that can assist anyone who desires to continue the journey to heaven. She colors her work with tips from the scriptures, from the works of the saints, and from her own experience of the spiritual life. She also included some reflective questions, and some practical tips for every chapter.

The book is a treasure for every Christian. I thank the writer immensely for this great work. I am therefore wasting no time in strongly and highly recommending the book to all, especially Christians. I believe it will be great nourishment to the spiritual life of all, and a vademecum for the preparation for heaven.

Nnaji, Damian (Fr)
Pontifical Lateran University, Rome.

Author's Note

Dear Reader,

As you embark on this journey through ABC of Making Heaven: A Blueprint for Earthly Success & Eternal Life, I invite you to open your heart to the transformative power of God's presence, Word, and grace. This is not just a book, it is a heartfelt offering, born from years of seeking, learning, and walking through the joys and trials of faith. It is a guide for those who yearn for a deeper relationship with God, a roadmap for navigating the Christian journey with clarity, purpose, and perseverance.

This book has been over fifteen years in the making, woven together from Scripture, personal experiences, and profound lessons learned in both triumph and suffering. Through it, I share insights that have shaped my understanding of God's love, His call to holiness, and the unwavering hope we have in His promises.

We live in a world filled with distractions and pressures that pull our hearts in countless directions, often clouding our sense of true purpose. But amidst the noise, God's voice remains steady, calling us to fix our eyes on what truly matters: a life anchored in Him.

Every chapter of this book is designed to help you shift your focus beyond the temporary and embrace the eternal, equipping you with the steps needed to align your life with God's will, featuring:

- Reflection on Scripture: Key Bible verses that illuminate the heart of each topic.
- Practical Steps: Clear, actionable ways to live out your faith daily.
- Reflection Questions: Thought-provoking prompts to guide personal growth and spiritual application.
- Prayers: Heartfelt supplications to draw you closer to God and invite His grace into your life.
- Real-Life Examples: Stories from Scripture, the lives of saints, and everyday experiences that inspire and encourage.

This book is not meant to be read passively. I encourage you to engage deeply, reflect, pray, and apply these principles to your life. The path to heaven is not meant to be walked alone; it is strengthened by the love, prayers, and support of a faith-filled community.

The journey to heaven is not easy. My prayer is that these pages stir within you a renewed hunger for holiness, a firmer trust in God's promises, and an unwavering commitment to walk this path with faith. May this book bring you hope in trials, courage in doubt, and assurance of God's presence always.

Thank you for allowing me to share this journey with you. May God's love and blessings be with you and your loved ones.

In Christ's love,
Uju Oramah

Introduction

Why This Book?

Imagine embarking on a journey where the destination is certain, yet only those who follow the right map will arrive. The map has always been available, laid out in Scripture and revealed through Christ's teachings, yet many lose their way simply because they never learned to navigate it. Others become distracted, following paths that seem easier, only to realize too late that they have wandered far from the truth.

As Scripture warns, "My people are destroyed for lack of knowledge" (Hosea 4:6). The path to heaven is not hidden, yet a lack of understanding keeps many from finding it. Salvation is not a passive inheritance but a deliberate pursuit.

One day, someone asked Jesus, "Lord, will only a few be saved?" His response was sobering: "Strive to enter through the narrow door, for many, I tell you, will try to enter and will not be able" (Luke 13:23-24). His words remind us that eternity is not secured by wishful thinking but by intentional living, striving, persevering, and choosing daily to walk the narrow path.

This book is for the Christian who longs for God, thirsts for righteousness, and desires to live in a way that pleases Him. It is a guide for those seeking clarity in their faith journey, providing wisdom and practical steps to grow in holiness and remain steadfast in a world that pulls us in the opposite direction.

Jesus said, "Strive first for the kingdom of God and His righteousness, and all these things will be given to you as well" (Matthew 6:33). The pursuit of God's kingdom should not be an afterthought. It must be our highest priority, the compass directing every aspect of our lives. By the end of this book, you will not only understand the path to eternal life but be equipped to walk it with confidence and purpose.

The Importance of an Eternal Perspective

Have you ever considered that every choice you make today echoes into eternity? We often live as though this world is all there is, caught up in the pursuit of success, comfort, and security. Yet Jesus posed a piercing question: "For what will it profit them to gain the whole world and forfeit their life?" (Mark 8:36).

Our time on earth is fleeting, a moment in the vastness of eternity. Our every thought, words, and action carry weight beyond this life. We should recognize that our daily choices shape not just our present but our forever. If heaven is our ultimate goal, it must shape our priorities, relationships, sacrifices, and faithfulness. It is the most worthwhile pursuit of all. As you turn these pages, may you find wisdom, strength, and encouragement to walk this path with unwavering faith.

Chapter 1

Knowledge of God: The Foundation of Everything

Have you ever felt a deep longing to truly know the One who created you? True knowledge of God is more than intellectual understanding; it is the foundation of your purpose and the key to a fulfilled and successful life. As the apostle Paul reminds us, " For 'In him we live and move and have our being." (Acts 17:28). God, our Creator and Sustainer, calls us into an intimate relationship with Him. A relationship that leads to both earthly success and eternal life.

To live a holy life, we must first understand who God is. His nature is revealed in Scripture:

- **Compassionate and Gracious:** God's mercy and kindness extend to us even when we don't deserve it. "The Lord is merciful and gracious, slow to anger and abounding in steadfast love." (Psalm 103:8).
- **Omnipotent:** God is all-powerful, with unlimited authority and ability. "Ah Lord God! It is you who made the heavens and the earth by your great power and by your outstretched arm! Nothing is too hard for you." (Jeremiah 32:17).
- **Omniscient:** God is all-knowing and fully aware of everything about us, our thoughts, actions, and

intentions. "O Lord, you have searched me and known me. You know when I sit down and when I rise up; you discern my thoughts from far away. You search out my path and my lying down and are acquainted with all my ways. Even before a word is on my tongue, O Lord, you know it completely." (Psalm 139:1-4).

- **Omnipresent:** God is always present everywhere; there is no place His Spirit cannot reach. "Where can I go from Your Spirit? Where can I flee from Your presence?" (Psalm 139:7-10).
- **Holy:** Holiness refers to God's absolute purity, perfection, and separation from sin. He calls us to be holy. "For I am the Lord your God; sanctify yourselves therefore, and be holy, for I am holy." (Leviticus 11:44-45).
- **Love:** At His core, God is love. His love is selfless, sacrificial, and unconditional, calling us to love others as He loves us. "Whoever does not love does not know God, for God is love." (1 John 4:8).

These attributes are not just theological concepts—they shape how we relate to God and live our lives. By growing in the awareness of His compassion, power, knowledge, presence, holiness, and love, we deepen our trust, reverence, and intimacy with Him.

As this transformation takes place, we become reflections of His grace and holiness, shining His light in a world longing for truth and hope.

Reflective Question:
Am I truly seeking to know God each day? Are there specific areas of my life where I am resisting His wisdom or love?

Practical Step: Cultivating Knowledge of God
1. **Daily Commitment:** Begin each day with a prayer for wisdom and revelation. Ask God to reveal more of Himself to you through His Word and experiences throughout the day.
2. **Bible Meditation:** Spend 15 minutes each day reflecting on verses that reveal God's attributes, such as Psalm 139, Jeremiah 32:17, and John 1:1-5.
3. **Reflection:** Consider how each of God's attributes influences your relationship with Him and how it should shape your daily decisions.

Prayer: Lord, I seek to know You more each day. Open my eyes to see Your hand in every part of my life. Draw me deeper into Your love and truth, and guide me to live in a way that glorifies You. Amen.

Closing Thoughts

By cultivating a deep knowledge of God, you lay a strong foundation for your spiritual journey. This knowledge is the beginning of a life rooted in His love, purpose, and power. Let this truth guide you as you continue your journey toward a closer relationship with the Divine.

CHAPTER 2

Knowledge of Self: Understanding Our Nature and Need for Grace

Have you ever tried to control every aspect of your life, only to feel everything slipping through your fingers? The frustration of repeated failures reveals a deeper truth about our human condition: we are limited and powerless against sin, Satan and his agents without God's grace.

We were created pure, reflecting God's image, but through Adam and Eve's disobedience, humanity fell from grace and inherited a sinful nature. As Scripture declares, "The LORD saw that the wickedness of humankind was great in the earth, and that every inclination of the thoughts of their hearts was only evil continually" (Genesis 6:5). This fallen state cannot be overcome by sheer willpower. The more we rely on ourselves, the more we stumble.

Grace: The Bridge to Transformation

The good news is that God, in His infinite mercy, did not leave us trapped in sin. Through Jesus Christ's sacrifice, He offers salvation and the grace to rise above our weaknesses. "For by grace you have been saved through faith, and this is not your own doing; it is the gift of God—not the result of works, so that no one may boast" (Ephesians 2:8-9).

I once believed I could manage everything on my own, striving for perfection through sheer determination. Each failure left me exhausted and disheartened. Only when I admitted my need for God's grace did things begin to change. Surrendering self-reliance transformed my failures into opportunities for growth. Now, when I fall, I lean on God's grace, knowing He will lift me up.

Embracing Our Dependence on God

Recognizing our need for God's grace is key to living a holy life. St. Paul reminds us, "All of us once lived among them in the passions of our flesh, following the desires of flesh and senses, and we were by nature children of wrath, like everyone else. But God, who is rich in mercy, out of the great love with which he loved us even when we were dead through our trespasses, made us alive together with Christ—by grace you have been saved" (Ephesians 2:3-5).

Once spiritually dead, we have been restored to life through Christ. Now, we are called to align our will with God's, for we were created to know, love, and serve Him.

Reflective Questions:
- How can acknowledging your need for God's grace change the way you approach daily challenges?
- In what specific areas of your life do you struggle with relying on your strength instead of trusting in God's grace?

- What steps can you take to remind yourself daily that God's grace is available to you, no matter your limitations and failures?

Practical Steps:
1. **Examine Your Heart Regularly:** Frequently assess your actions, thoughts, and motives by asking yourself, "Am I living in alignment with God's will?" Reflect honestly on your dependence on God and Seek His guidance to correct any missteps.
2. **Daily Confession and Repentance:** Cultivate a habit of daily confession and sincere repentance. Acknowledge your sins, ask for forgiveness, and make a conscious effort to turn away from them. This practice helps you embrace grace and stay grounded in God's mercy.
3. **Seek the Sacraments:** If you are Catholic, prioritize regular confession and the Eucharist. St. Padre Pio wisely counseled, "Confession is the soul's bath... for even a clean room gathers dust, and so does the soul." Aim for frequent confession to cleanse your heart and renew your commitment to holiness.
4. **Acknowledge Your Weakness and Trust in God's Strength:** Remember St. Paul's words: "Therefore I am content with weaknesses, insults, hardships, persecutions, and calamities for the sake of Christ; for whenever I am weak, then I am strong." (2 Corinthians 12:10). Embrace your limitations with humility and rely on God's power to sustain you through your challenges.
5. **Engage in Daily Surrender Prayer:** Each morning, pray a short prayer of surrender, such as:

"Lord, I cannot do this on my own. I need Your grace to guide me, strengthen me, and sustain me."

Prayer: Psalm 51

Pray Psalm 51 as a heartfelt plea for mercy and renewal: "Create in me a clean heart, O God, and renew a right spirit within me" (Psalm 51:10).

This powerful prayer of repentance invites you to acknowledge your sins, seek God's forgiveness, and receive His grace for transformation.

Closing Thoughts:

By adopting these steps, you will cultivate a deeper understanding of yourself and a greater reliance on God's grace. Recognizing your fallen nature, acknowledging your weaknesses, and surrendering to God's strength form the foundation of true spiritual growth and holiness. Transformation happens when you let go of self-reliance and fully embrace God's grace, allowing His power to work through you. In doing so, you will discover the strength to walk confidently in His light, no matter the challenges you face.

Let God's grace be your guide, and His strength will sustain you on the journey toward holiness and eternal life.

Chapter 3

Embracing Humility: The Gateway to God's Grace

The Essence of Humility

What would your life look like if you stopped measuring success by your achievements and instead trusted God with each step? Humility is the foundation of all virtues. It is an honest recognition of who we truly are in God. It involves acknowledging our limitations, weaknesses, and dependence on His grace.

As St. Teresa of Ávila wisely said, "Humility is the foundation of all virtues; in humility alone can the grace of God be found." Just as rich soil nourishes seeds, humility nurtures our spirit. It makes room for God's grace to transform us.

Humility isn't about thinking less of ourselves, but seeing ourselves rightly. It is recognizing that while we are loved and valued by God, we are not self-sufficient. True humility keeps us grounded, helps us rely on God's strength, and frees us from the exhausting need for self-justification.

The Biblical Perspective on Humility

The Bible is filled with teachings on humility. Jesus Christ demonstrated the ultimate humility by leaving His heavenly throne and taking on human form. Consider Philippians 2:5-8:

"Let the same mind be in you that was in Christ Jesus, who, though he was in the form of God, did not regard equality with God as something to be exploited, but emptied himself, taking the form of a slave, being born in human likeness. And being found in human form, he humbled himself and became obedient to the point of death— even death on a cross."

Jesus' humility was not weakness; it was strength under God's control. As His followers, we are called to embody the same humility, not by diminishing ourselves, but by exalting God through our lives. Humility aligns us with God's will and invites His grace to work through us. (Philippians 2:5-8)

The Transformative Power of Humility

Humility is transformative. When we humble ourselves, we shift from self-reliance to God-reliance. This opens the door to spiritual growth, deeper intimacy with God, and a greater capacity to love others. James 4:10 reminds us, "Humble yourselves before the Lord, and He will lift you up."

Humility reshapes our relationships with others. It softens our hearts, making us more compassionate, patient, and forgiving. It frees us from pride, envy, and comparison. Instead of seeing life as a competition, we begin to see it as a shared journey toward God's kingdom.

Through humility, we become the people God created us to be, open, receptive, and fully dependent on His grace. Living humbly is an ongoing process of self-examination, surrender, and service.

A Biblical Example: The Pharisee and the Tax Collector

In **Luke 18:9-14**, Jesus tells the parable of the Pharisee and the tax collector. The Pharisee, full of pride, prayed, "God, I thank you that I am not like other people... I fast twice a week and give a tenth of all I get." In contrast, the tax collector, overwhelmed by his unworthiness, prayed, "'God, have mercy on me, a sinner."

Jesus concluded, "I tell you that this man, rather than the other, went home justified before God. For all those who exalt themselves will be humbled, and those who humble themselves will be exalted."

This parable is a sobering reminder to reject self-righteousness and embrace humble dependence on God. It challenges us to examine our hearts: Are we exalting ourselves or surrendering to God's mercy? Do we recognize that everything we are, our intellect, influence, and abilities, is a gift from God? And do we always give Him the glory?

My Journey of Humility

I once believed that my successes were the result of my hard work alone. I leaned heavily on my abilities, convinced that my effort was the key to every achievement. But when life brought setbacks, my confidence shattered. One particular failure left me feeling lost and defeated. In that moment of despair, the Holy Spirit opened my eyes; I had been relying on my own strength instead of God's.

That realization changed everything. Now, even in failure, I remind myself that God makes all things good and new: "We know that all things work together for good for those who love

God, who are called according to his purpose" (Romans 8:28). He can bring beauty even from my brokenness. This truth has freed me from self-condemnation, shifting my heart to trust in God's mercy and transformative power.

Humbled, I turned to God in prayer, confessing my need for His grace. As I surrendered my pride, a profound peace washed over me. The more I acknowledged my dependence on Him, the more I felt His presence guiding me. This journey of humility transformed not just my actions, but my heart. I came to understand that true strength is not found in self-reliance, but in fully trusting God.

The Role of the Holy Spirit

The Holy Spirit is essential in cultivating humility. He convicts us of pride, empowers us to change, and gently guides us toward a life that honors God. Through His quiet nudges and inner promptings, the Holy Spirit reminds us that true strength is found in humility.

By yielding to the Spirit, we experience the transformative power of humility. We learn to forgo our need for control and embrace God's grace in every aspect of life.

Reflection Questions
- How have you experienced the transformative power of humility in your life?
- In what areas are you still relying on your strength instead of God's?

- What steps can you take to surrender your self-righteousness and draw closer to God through humility?

Practical Steps to Cultivate Humility
1. **Self-Reflection**: Regularly examine your thoughts and actions. Ask the Holy Spirit to reveal areas of pride and lead you toward humility.
2. **Sincere Confession**: Admit your pride to God and seek His forgiveness. Recognize your dependence on His grace.
3. **Practice Gratitude**: Thank God for His blessings. Gratitude shifts focus from yourself to God's goodness.
4. **Serve Others**: Selflessly serve those around you, imitating Christ's humility.
5. **Embrace Correction**: Be open to feedback, viewing it as a chance to grow.
6. **Grounded in Scripture**: Let God's Word shape your heart and mind. Reflect on passages that encourage humility.
7. **Pray for Humility**: Ask God to help you cultivate a humble heart and rely more on Him.

Prayer: Psalm 131

Pray with the words of **Psalm 131**: "O Lord, my heart is not lifted up; my eyes are not raised too high; I do not occupy myself with things too great and too marvelous for me. But I have calmed and quieted my soul, like a weaned child with its mother; like a weaned child is my soul within me". Let these words guide you toward childlike trust and humility before God.

Closing Thoughts

Humility is more than a virtue; it's a way of life that draws us closer to God. By surrendering our pride, we create space for God's grace to work in us. Through humility, we find purpose, peace, and strength in God's loving presence.

Chapter 4

What God Loves: Living a Life That Pleases Him

What if God's joy lies not in grand achievements, but in the quiet devotion of our daily lives? Could it be that small, consistent acts of love are the true treasures we offer Him? God's desire for us is clear: to live in holiness and righteousness. The Bible reveals that God values obedience, humility, and love—first directed toward Him, and then extended to others. As Jesus said, "If you love me, keep my commandments" (John 14:15). Genuine love for God is reflected through our actions, not just our words.

A Heartfelt Realization

I once believed that pleasing God required extraordinary sacrifices or intense displays of devotion. I thought that to honor Him, my faith had to be marked by grand gestures. But through immersing myself in Scripture, attending spiritual retreats, and engaging with fellow believers, I had a profound realization that God delights in the simple, everyday acts of obedience and love.

Offering our work, our rest, and even our struggles to Him can be a powerful form of worship. This shift in perspective transformed my faith. I began to see that it's the small, consistent actions, like a quiet prayer, a kind word, or a moment of gratitude, that draw us deeper into God's presence.

Examples of Saints

Just as I discovered the beauty in simple acts of love, saints like St. Thérèse of Lisieux, St. Alphonsus, and St. John of the Cross demonstrated that holiness is found in the ordinary moments of life.

St. Thérèse, known for her "little way," taught that doing small things with great love is the key to holiness. Her childlike trust and simplicity remind us that every humble action can be an offering to God.

St. John of the Cross, who endured immense suffering, found joy and peace in knowing that his trials brought him closer to Christ. He shows us that even in pain, God's presence and love are near when we surrender to His will.

In his book, Uniformity with the Will of God, St. Alphonsus said, "Perfection is founded entirely on the love of God...and perfect love of God means the complete union of our will with God's." His words reflect Jesus' teaching: "If you love me, keep my commandments" (John 14:15).

These saints remind us that holiness isn't reserved for grand gestures or major life events. Rather, it's found in the day-to-day choices to practice humility, patience, and joy as we embrace God's will.

Reflection Questions

- Can you recall a time when your obedience brought you closer to God? How did it strengthen your faith?
- How can you bring more humility and love into your everyday actions?

- What are small but impactful ways you can show love to those around you, knowing it pleases God?

Practical Steps: Living a Life That Pleases God
1. **Commit to Daily Obedience:**
   Choose one specific area, patience, kindness, or humility, where you will practice intentional obedience each day.
   Example: In a moment of frustration, you can choose to remain calm and speak with kindness instead of reacting in anger.
2. **Cultivate a Heart of Gratitude:**
   Gratitude shifts your focus from what you lack to the abundance of God's blessings. Start each morning or end each evening by listing three things you're thankful for, no matter how small.
   Example: Thank God for the breath you take, the food on your table, or the love of family and friends.
3. **Engage in Regular Self-Examination:**
   Reflect on your day by asking: "Did my actions today align with God's love?" Pray for the grace to grow in areas where you struggle. Keep a journal to track your progress and identify opportunities to surrender more fully to God.

Prayer: Psalm 86
O Lord, teach me to see Your will in every moment and help me to walk in daily humility, gratitude, and love. Guide me toward actions that bring You joy, even in the unnoticed acts

of love. May my heart always seek to please You in the small choices I make each day.

Closing Thoughts

By choosing love, gratitude, and obedience each day, you align yourself with God's heart. Remember, it is often in the quiet, unnoticed acts of love that we bring the greatest joy to God and open ourselves to His abundant blessings. Through these daily practices, you will grow in holiness, cultivating a life that is truly pleasing to Him.

Chapter 5

God's Dislikes: What Offends God and What He Calls Us to Avoid

A Heart That Honors God

Have you ever felt the sting of regret after disappointing someone close to you? Imagine how much deeper our pain should be when our actions grieve the heart of God if we love Him. Recognizing what offends Him is essential for living a life that honors Him. As Proverbs 9:10 teaches: "The fear of the LORD is the beginning of wisdom, and the knowledge of the Holy One is insight."

Understanding God's holiness and what displeases Him helps us align our hearts with His will. When we know His dislikes, we gain wisdom and the strength to walk in righteousness.

A Personal Awakening

In my younger years, I overlooked the virtue of patience, seeing it as unimportant. I believed life was meant to be lived quickly, with little regard for qualities that seemed to slow me down. However, my impatience led me to make choices that, without realizing it, offended God and caused me to lose valuable opportunities, true friends, and destiny helpers.

When I began immersing myself in Scripture and learning from the lives of the saints, the Holy Spirit convicted me, revealing areas of my life that needed change. I came to understand that patience is not just a virtue but a path to holiness and breakthrough. This realization transformed me. I learned that avoiding sin isn't merely about saying "no" to wrongdoing; it's about actively aligning every aspect of my life with God's will.

God's Holiness: The Standard for Our Lives

God's holiness is the standard by which we are called to live. The Lord commands, "For I am the LORD who brought you up from the land of Egypt to be your God; you shall be holy, for I am holy" (Leviticus 11:45). This command is not merely an ideal to aspire to but a call to reflect God's character in our daily lives. In a world filled with distractions and temptations, striving for holiness keeps us aligned with God's heart and ensures true success in life. To achieve this, we must understand what grieves Him and actively turn away from it.

What Offends God

God's Word outlines attitudes and behaviors that offend Him. These actions not only harm our relationship with God but also hinder our spiritual growth, and the ability to become another Christ in the world.

1. **Idolatry:** Placing anything or anyone above God. "You shall have no other gods before me" (Exodus 20:3-4).
   Idolatry is not just worshiping false gods, it's putting anything (work, wealth, relationships) above God. It leaves our souls empty and vulnerable.
2. **Pride: Trusting in Ourselves Instead of God**
   "Pride goes before destruction, and a haughty spirit before a fall" (Proverbs 16:18). Pride blinds us to our

need for God. It builds a barrier that prevents us from experiencing a deeper, personal knowledge of God.
3. **Injustice:** Mistreating Others- "Learn to do good; seek justice, rescue the oppressed, defend the orphan, plead for the widow." (Isaiah 1:17). God is deeply offended by unfairness, especially when it leads to the oppression of the vulnerable.
4. **Sexual Immorality:** Engaging in sexual behavior outside God's design for marriage. "Shun fornication!... your body is a temple of the Holy Spirit" (1 Corinthians 6:18-20). Misusing God's design for sexuality damages our relationship with Him and distorts our view of love.
5. **Deceit and Lying:** Distorting the Truth.
"Lying lips are an abomination to the Lord"(Proverbs 12:22). Deceit breaks trust and is contrary to God's nature as the God of truth.
6. **Disobedience to God's Commandments:**
"If you love me, keep my commandments"(John 14:15). Willful disobedience disrupts our fellowship with God and undermines His authority over us.

Lessons from King David's Life
King David's story serves as a profound reminder of the devastating consequences of sin and the transformative power of true repentance. Though known as "a man after God's own heart," David's sin with Bathsheba and his killing of Uriah deeply grieved God (2 Samuel 11–12). Yet when David sincerely repented, God restored him.

This shows us that while sin offends God, sincere repentance leads to His forgiveness and healing and restoration.

Reflection Questions
- **What areas of your life might be offending God?**
  Reflect on choices or attitudes that distance you from Him.
- **What practical steps can you take today to realign with God's will?**
  Identify one specific action you need to change.
- **How can understanding what offends God influence your daily choices?**
  Consider one habit you can change to honor Him more.

Practical Steps: Avoiding What Offends God
1. **Examine Your Conscience Regularly**
   Take 10 minutes each night to reflect: "Did my actions please or offend God today?" Confess any sins and ask for grace to improve.
2. **Repent Quickly**
   When you recognize sin, turn to God immediately. "If we confess our sins, he who is faithful and just will forgive us our sins and cleanse us from all unrighteousness." (1 John 1:9).
3. **Avoid Occasions of Sin**
   Identify situations that lead to sin and take steps to avoid them. For example, if anger tempts you, pause and pray before responding.
4. **Renew Your Mind with Scripture.**
   Regularly read the Bible to understand God's heart and align with His will. "Do not be conformed to this world,

but be transformed by the renewing of your minds, so that you may discern what is the will of God—what is good and acceptable and perfect." (Romans 12:2).

5. **Seek Accountability and Fellowship**
   Surround yourself with people who encourage righteous living. "Iron sharpens iron" (Proverbs 27:17).
6. **Pray for a Heart That Hates Sin**
   Ask God to help you detest sin and love His ways.

Prayer

Lord, help me to love what You love and to hate what displeases You. Give me the strength to live in a way that honors You. In Jesus' name, amen.

Suggested Psalms for Prayer:

Consider praying these Psalms, which express sorrow over sin and seek God's mercy:

- **Psalm 6**: A cry for mercy in the face of deep distress.
- **Psalm 32**: A prayer of repentance, acknowledging the joy of forgiveness.
- **Psalm 38**: A plea for healing and deliverance from sin.
- **Psalm 51**: David's prayer of repentance after his sin with Bathsheba.
- **Psalm 102**: A prayer for God's mercy in times of affliction.
- **Psalm 130**: A cry for mercy, emphasizing hope in God's redemption.
- **Psalm 143**: A prayer for guidance and deliverance from trouble.

Closing Thoughts
Avoiding what offends God is not a burden but a pathway to joy and freedom. Through humility, repentance, and obedience, we grow closer to His heart. Remember, each day is an opportunity to align your life with God's holiness and receive His endless grace.

Chapter 6

Repentance and Forgiveness: Pathways to Healing and Renewal

What is Repentance? Repentance means recognizing your sins, feeling genuine sorrow for them, and deciding to turn away from sin to follow God's will. It's more than just regret; it involves a change of heart and behavior. True repentance leads to asking for forgiveness and committing yourself to a renewed, faithful life.

Repentance is both an act of humility and a response to God's grace. As Scripture says, "Bear fruit worthy of repentance." (Matthew 3:8). This means that genuine repentance is reflected not only in our words but also in transformed actions. It's not a one-time event but a continuous journey, a daily choice to realign our hearts with God's will.

Repentance invites us to let God's Spirit reshape our thoughts, desires, and behaviors. Through constant self-examination and a willingness to grow, we open the door to lasting renewal.

Forgiveness: A Divine Gift and a Sacred Command

Forgiveness is choosing to let go of anger and resentment toward someone who has wronged you, giving yourself the freedom to heal and move forward. It lies at the heart of the Christian life. It is a precious gift from God, who cleanses us from sin, and a sacred command we are called to follow. Jesus highlighted the boundless nature of forgiveness when He taught us to forgive "seventy-seven times" (Matthew 18:22). This profound teaching reminds us that just as God offers us endless mercy, we are called to extend the same mercy to others.

Forgiving others can be challenging, especially when the wounds are deep. Yet, forgiveness is essential for our spiritual freedom. It liberates us from the chains of bitterness, anger, and resentment. True forgiveness does not mean excusing the wrong done to us; instead, it means choosing to let go and allowing our hearts to be free from the grip of negativity.

When we forgive, we create space for God's healing grace and peace to flow into our lives. By forgiving, we mirror God's love and open ourselves to His blessings and His transformative power. We thus find true freedom and inner peace.

The Transformative Power of Repentance and Forgiveness

Why Repentance Heals: Repentance renews our relationship with God. When we humbly acknowledge our sins and seek His forgiveness, we experience spiritual healing and restoration. The prophet Isaiah declares, "Though your sins are like scarlet, they shall be like snow" (Isaiah 1:18). God's forgiveness cleanses us, removing guilt and shame, and allows us to walk in true freedom and the fullness of His blessings.

Why Forgiveness Heals

Forgiveness heals relationships and brings peace to our souls. Holding on to anger or resentment creates spiritual and emotional barriers. By choosing to forgive, we release these burdens and allow God's grace to mend what is broken. As the Apostle Paul reminds us, "Be kind to one another, tenderhearted, forgiving one another, as God in Christ forgave you" (Ephesians 4:32).

The Parable of the Unforgiving Servant

Jesus powerfully illustrated the importance of forgiveness in the Parable of the Unforgiving Servant (Matthew 18:21-35). In this story, a servant owed an enormous debt to a king, a debt he could never repay. Out of compassion, the king forgave the entire debt. However, this same servant refused to forgive a fellow servant who owed him a much smaller sum. The king, angered by his lack of mercy, revoked his forgiveness and punished him.

This parable serves as a solemn warning: when we withhold forgiveness, we hinder the flow of God's mercy in our own lives. As recipients of His boundless mercy and forgiveness, we are called to extend the same to others.

The Role of the Holy Spirit

The Holy Spirit empowers our journey of repentance and forgiveness. He plays a vital role in helping us:

- **Recognize Sin**: The Holy Spirit convinces us gently, revealing areas in our lives that need transformation.
- **Empower Change**: He gives us the strength to turn from sin and walk in righteousness.

- **Enable Forgiveness**: The Spirit softens our hearts, helping us to forgive others and release resentment.
- Through the Holy Spirit's guidance, we grow in holiness and experience the fullness of God's love and freedom.

Reflection Questions
- How has practicing forgiveness deepened your relationship with God and others?
- What steps can you take to make repentance and forgiveness a daily habit?
- Is there someone you need to forgive today? How can you take the first step toward reconciliation?

Practical Steps for Genuine Repentance and Forgiveness
1. Daily Self-Examination: Reflect on your actions at the end of each day. Ask the Holy Spirit to show you where repentance or forgiveness is needed.
2. Practice Humility: Acknowledge your need for God's mercy. "God opposes the proud but gives grace to the humble" (James 4:6).
3. Confess Sincerely: Confess your sins to God with genuine remorse and resolve to change.
4. Engage in the Sacrament of Confession: If you are Catholic, regularly participate in confession. This sacrament offers grace and spiritual renewal.
5. Forgive Actively: Make a conscious choice to forgive those who have wronged you, trusting God to heal any bitterness. Seek reconciliation whenever possible.

6. Pray for Grace: Ask God to help you cultivate a heart that loves holiness and detests sin. Also, meditate on the contrition expressed in Psalm 6.

Closing Thoughts

Repentance and forgiveness are the gateways to healing, freedom, and a renewed relationship with God. When we practice the above, we open ourselves to God's transformative power. As we commit to these pathways, we will experience peace, love, and the joy of living in harmony with God's will.

Chapter 7

Tribulations: The Refining Process Toward Holiness

Shaped by the Sculptor's Hand

Have you ever felt that life's challenges are too overwhelming to endure? Imagine yourself as a block of marble, with God as the sculptor. Every trial, every hardship, is a deliberate chisel stroke revealing the masterpiece within you. Trials are not interruptions to a peaceful life; they are essential to your Christian journey. Just as weights in a gym build physical strength, challenges build spiritual resilience, refine your character, and draw you closer to God.

Scripture assures us that God uses difficulties to shape us into His image: "Consider it pure joy, my brothers and sisters, whenever you face trials of many kinds, because you know that the testing of your faith produces perseverance" (James 1:2-3). Therefore, trials are not meant to break you but to refine you. What if your current struggle is God's tool, preparing you to become the person He designed you to be?

Forged by Fire: My Walk with God

Years ago, I faced what felt like a "Dark Night of the Soul," a period when I felt completely abandoned by God. After graduation from college in Nigeria, I spent five years searching for a job. Despite persistent prayers and faith, every opportunity that came my way had conditions that conflicted with my beliefs. With each "no," the isolation and frustration I felt deepened. At home, I became the family's main support system, shouldering responsibilities others couldn't bear as they worked or attended school.

The breaking point came during a family emergency that forced me to miss a rare career convention in Abuja. The event could have opened doors to potential employers, but the opportunity slipped away. Missing that opportunity left me feeling as if my last hope had vanished. In my despair, I reached a point where prayer felt pointless. I told God I was done. I felt as though He had taken advantage of my love and trust.

Yet, even in that darkness, God was silently at work. My spiritual director, who visited my city only once a year, happened to be available. I poured out my frustrations to him. He listened to my frustrations and shared his own story of faith, which included profound suffering and disappointments, including the recent loss of his sibling's only child, a university student.

His burdens were heavier than mine. Yet, despite his grief, his faith remained unshaken. His resilience ignited a flicker of hope in me. I realized that I was not alone and found renewed strength to continue on my path.

The numbness I felt toward God didn't lift immediately, but within a few months, I began to experience joy in worship again. Looking back, I see God's grace sustaining me. Years before, I had been advised to visit the Blessed Sacrament regularly and pray for perseverance. Little did I know those visits were laying a foundation of strength I would desperately need.

God's preparation often precedes our trials, equipping us with unseen grace. Even when we cannot feel His presence, He is near, chiseling away, transforming us through the fire of tribulation.

Purpose of the Tribulations
Trials are not evidence of God's absence; they are tools to reveal His purpose. The Bible overflows with stories of God's faithful servants who endured great hardships yet found God present through it all.
- **Job's Suffering and Restoration**: Job lost everything—wealth, health, and family. In his grief and confusion, he still trusted God's plan. His endurance led to restoration and greater blessings (Job 42:10-17).
- **Paul's Perseverance**: St. Paul faced imprisonment, beatings, and shipwrecks. Yet he saw trials as opportunities to grow in faith and advance the gospel: "Everything that was written in the past was written to teach us" (Romans 15:4).

These examples remind us that suffering is a tool in God's hands, purifying our intentions, strengthening our resolve, and drawing us closer to Him. It also matures us, preparing us to embrace the mantle He destined for us before we were born.

Even in our darkest moments, we have this assurance: "We know that all things work together for good for those who love God, who are called according to his purpose." (Romans 8:28)

Reflection Questions:
- Think of a recent trial that tested your faith. How did it shape your relationship with God?

- How can you approach future challenges with a mindset of growth and trust in God's purpose?

Practical Steps: Embracing Tribulations as a Path to Holiness
1. **Acknowledge God's Purpose in Trials**
   Instead of resisting challenges, choose to see them as opportunities for growth. Ask God to reveal His purpose in your struggles and reflect on Christ's suffering and perseverance.
2. **Immerse Yourself in Scripture**
   Meditate on passages that highlight God's faithfulness during trials. Let His Word renew your hope and remind you that He is with you through every storm.
3. **Seek Support from Fellow Believers**
   Lean on your faith community for encouragement. Trusted friends, spiritual mentors, and prayer partners can provide perspective and strength during difficult times.
4. **Praise God Amidst Trials**
   Worship redirects your focus from your problem to God's power. Paul and Silas sang hymns in prison, and their praise led to miraculous deliverance (Acts 16:25-26). Praise invites God's presence into your struggle and renews your spirit.
5. Create a playlist of worship songs that remind you of God's love and faithfulness. Let praise be your weapon against despair, transforming trials into opportunities to glorify God.

Closing Thoughts

Every trial has an end, and through each one, God is drawing you closer to Him. Tribulations refine your faith, build resilience, and prepare you for both earthly victory and eternity in God's presence. By embracing challenges with trust and perseverance, you will gain strength, peace, and a deeper intimacy with God that surpasses all understanding. You will also acquire wisdom that could only come from what you have endured, the fruit of your suffering. "Blessed is anyone who endures temptation. Such a one has stood the test and will receive the crown of life that the Lord has promised to those who love him" (James 1:12).

Chapter 8

Self-Deliverance and Spiritual Warfare – Walking in the Light of Christ

My Personal Story:

I once believed that deliverance was only necessary for those facing extreme spiritual struggles. But one midnight prayer session shattered that misconception. Out of nowhere, I felt overwhelming heaviness, as if fear itself had wrapped around me, suffocating my spirit. My words were trapped, but my heart cried out silently to Jesus. The oppressive presence receded for a moment but returned as I continued to pray. By the fifth encounter, I realized I was in a serious spiritual battle.

Recalling an exorcism prayer by St. Anthony of Padua that my spiritual director had recommended, I grabbed my phone, searched online, and found the prayer. With trembling faith, I prayed three times, making the sign of the cross with each repetition:

"Behold the Cross of the Lord! Begone, you evil powers! The Lion of the tribe of Judah, the root of David, has conquered Alleluia!"

As I prayed, a profound peace filled the room, and the oppressive presence lifted. Finally, I could complete my prayers, undisturbed and strengthened by God's presence.

That night taught me a crucial lesson: we must be spiritually prepared to face challenges, whether physical or spiritual. As St. Paul urges in Ephesians 6:11, "Put on the whole armor of God, so that you may be able to stand against the wiles of the devil." God's power equips us to confront spiritual opposition with confidence. By inviting Christ's light, His Word, and His character into every aspect of our lives, we are strengthened against darkness and empowered to walk in victory.

The Victory We Have in Christ: Walking in His Light
Believers have the assurance of victory through Jesus Christ. Scripture declares, "Little children, you are from God and have overcome them; for the one who is in you is greater than the one who is in the world" (1 John 4:4).

But do we truly know how to respond when our lives come under attack? What about when our hearts convict us of sin? Or when we find ourselves in trouble with no hope or help in sight?

The answers are found throughout Scripture. In their darkest moments, King David, Daniel, and many others turned to God and triumphed through His power. Their stories reveal the spiritual weapons available to us—if we seek them with open hearts.

Through His death and resurrection, Jesus Christ secured our victory and gave us authority over spiritual darkness. This victory is not a distant hope; it is a present reality. Walking in

Christ's light transforms how we live, empowering us to overcome temptation, experience deliverance, and walk in true freedom. As Matthew 4:16 proclaims, "The people who sat in darkness have seen a great light."

Walking in His light is about relationships, not ritual. Consider Peter—once impulsive and weak in faith—who became a pillar of strength, healing others even with his shadow (Acts 5:15). Likewise, Saul's transformation into Paul made him a powerful vessel through whom God worked miracles; even his handkerchiefs brought healing (Acts 19:11-12). Their lives demonstrate that Christ's light empowers all who align with Him to reflect God's glory.

We actively seek Christ's light through self-deliverance, immersing ourselves in God's Word, praying for guidance, and daily inviting the Holy Spirit to transform us. By putting God's Word into action and making it our way of life, we step into the victory that God has already secured for us.

Understanding Spiritual Warfare

We must acknowledge the reality of spiritual warfare. Our struggles are not merely against human opposition but against powerful spiritual forces. Ephesians 6:12 warns us: "For our struggle is not against flesh and blood, but against the rulers, against the authorities, against the powers of this dark world and against the spiritual forces of evil in the heavenly places." St. Peter adds, "Discipline yourselves, keep alert. Like a roaring lion your adversary the devil prowls around, looking for someone to devour" (1 Peter 5:8).

The enemy's goal is to undermine our faith and disconnect us from God's power and benefits. Recognizing this battle equips us to stand firm in God.

Equipping for Battle: The Armor of God
Ephesians 6:10-18 outlines essential armor for spiritual warfare:
- **The Belt of Truth:** Put yourself in God's truth to counter the enemy's lies. For example, you can declare, "The Lord is my shepherd, I shall not want" (Psalm 23:1) and other promises God has spoken over you. Repeat them until they take root in your heart, shaping your beliefs and actions, regardless of the challenges you face.
- **The Breastplate of Righteousness:** Guard your heart by living in righteousness. Focus on cultivating the fruits of the Holy Spirit in your life which are love, joy, peace, patience, kindness, generosity, faithfulness, gentleness, and self-control (Galatians 5:22-23). These virtues shape your character, align your actions with God's will, and shield you from the enemy's attacks.
- **The Gospel of Peace:** Stand firm in the peace from knowing Christ's sacrifice and promises.
- **The Shield of Faith:** Trust God to protect you from the enemy's attacks.
- **The Helmet of Salvation:** Protect your mind with the assurance of salvation.
- **The Sword of the Spirit:** Wield God's Word to combat spiritual assaults. Scripture is powerful, memorize it and

declare it whenever negative thoughts or challenging situations arise. Just as Jesus overcame temptation by saying, "It is written" (Matthew 4:4), we too must speak God's truth over our lives, silencing lies and defeating the enemy's schemes.
- **Prayer:** Stay vigilant, praying in the Spirit on all occasions. Learn the art of constant communication with God; it is always your lifeline, in every situation. Just as breathing sustains physical life, unceasing prayer sustains your spiritual strength, keeping you connected to God's wisdom, guidance, and protection.

These are not just symbols; they are practical defenses. As highlighted in Chapter 5: God's Dislikes, avoiding sin and living righteously are vital to remaining vigilant and protected.

Fasting for Spiritual Breakthrough

During a season of spiritual siege, I fasted and prayed for clarity. Strongholds crumbled, and peace filled my heart. I gained insight into God's purpose for me. As Scripture reveals, "Then Jesus was led up by the Spirit into the wilderness to be tempted by the devil. He fasted forty days and forty nights, and afterward he was famished" (Matthew 4:1-2). This highlights the importance of fasting before beginning ministry, as it prepared Jesus spiritually for the mission ahead.

Fasting shifts our focus from physical needs to spiritual growth, making space for God's power to work within us. It is an act of surrender and deep reliance on Him, opening doors to renewal, divine revelation, and victory over spiritual battles.

Reflection Questions
- How have you experienced spiritual warfare, and how did you stand firm?
- In what ways can fasting and prayer deepen your connection with God?
- Are there areas in your life under spiritual attack where you need God's light to shine?

Practical Steps for Self-Deliverance and Spiritual Warfare
1. Daily Spiritual Cleansing: Ask for God's grace to renew and protect you.
2. Immerse in Scripture: Declare God's promises to dispel doubts and fears.
3. Wear the Armor of God: Visualize putting on each piece daily.
4. Incorporate Fasting: Dedicate specific times to fasting and seeking breakthroughs.
5. Pray Consistently: Cultivate a habit of seeking God's protection and strength.
6. Stay Vigilant: Be alert to the enemy's schemes and resist them.
7. Seek Community Support: Surround yourself with believers who encourage and pray with you.

These steps, combined with earlier disciplines of prayer and vigilance against sin create a resilient spiritual foundation.

Suggested Prayers
- **Psalm 18:** A prayer of deliverance.

- **Psalm 16:** A declaration of trust in God.
- **Psalm 35:** A plea for divine protection against enemies.

Closing Thoughts

By practicing these disciplines, you will grow in Christ's light, experience His deliverance, and be empowered to walk daily in the Spirit. Victory in Christ is not just a hope, it is a reality we are invited to live.

Chapter 9

Pray Without Ceasing: Your Lifeline to God

The Power of Unceasing Prayer

Imagine maintaining a close friendship where you only speak occasionally. How deep could that relationship truly grow? Our connection with God is no different. Prayer is the steady, heartfelt communication that nourishes and deepens our relationship with Him. It aligns us with His will, fills us with His wisdom, and equips us with His grace. Just as the sun nourishes plants, prayer does much more—it nurtures our spirit and strengthens our faith.

In 1 Thessalonians 5:17, Paul exhorts us to "pray without ceasing." This call invites us to view prayer as more than just a ritual; it's an ongoing, life-giving conversation with our Creator. When prayer becomes as natural as breathing, we remain anchored in God's presence, drawing ceaseless blessings, strength, and peace, no matter the circumstances. Without prayer, our spiritual life weakens; with it, we thrive.

Jesus Himself modeled this perfectly. He often withdrew to solitary places to pray (Luke 5:16). His consistent communion with the Father was the source of His strength. If Jesus relied on prayer, how much more do we need it to navigate our own lives?

A Personal Testimony: Discovering God's Direction Through Prayer

There was a season when I faced a daunting series of decisions. Initially, I turned to the internet, friends, and family for advice, but their suggestions left me restless. Frustration and confusion grew until I recalled a talk about seeking God first in all things, no matter how small.

Determined to trust God fully, I committed to prayer and fasting, surrendering my worries and asking for His guidance. As I prayed, clarity gradually emerged. Sometimes, it came as a sudden insight during prayer, other times, through dreams or quiet convictions. What once felt like a maze of confusion became a well-lit path.

This experience taught me that unceasing, heartfelt prayer isn't just about seeking answers, it's about aligning with God's timing, resting in His peace, and trusting His wisdom.

Reflection Questions

- How has prayer transformed your approach to life's challenges?
- What practical steps can you take to integrate prayer more fully into your daily routine?
- In what areas of your life do you need to trust God more deeply through prayer?

Practical Steps for Cultivating a Life of Unceasing Prayer

1. **Set Regular Prayer Times:** Establish a rhythm of prayer throughout your day. Just as you schedule meals or essential tasks, dedicate specific moments for

focused prayer. Start and end your day with prayer and integrate short prayers into daily activities. Simple phrases like "Lord, guide me," "Jesus, I trust in You," or "Thank You, Lord," can keep your mind and heart fixed on God.

2. **Incorporate Thanksgiving:** Gratitude is the foundation of a rich prayer life. Regularly thank God for His blessings, both big and small. Even during trials, thanking God shifts your perspective from lack to abundance and reinforces your faith. As Philippians 4:6 reminds us: "Do not worry about anything, but in everything by prayer and supplication with thanksgiving let your requests be made known to God."

3. **Practice Silent Prayer:** Cultivate moments of stillness to listen for God's voice. Silent prayer allows space for His gentle whisper, like the "still, small voice" Elijah heard (1 Kings 19:12). In a world of noise, these quiet times become sacred opportunities to hear God's guidance and experience His presence.

4. **Pray with Scripture:** Use God's Word to enrich your prayers. The Psalms offer prayers for every emotion: praise, lament, thanksgiving, and trust. Incorporating Scripture anchors your thoughts in truth. For instance, pray Psalm 23 when you need reassurance or Psalm 51 when seeking forgiveness.

5. **Pray During Everyday Tasks:** Transform mundane activities into moments of connection with God. Whether washing dishes, driving, or walking, use these

times for short prayers. Invite God into your daily routines, making each moment a silent act of worship.

Closing Thoughts

When you cultivate unceasing prayer, you anchor your life in God's love, wisdom, and peace. This constant communion not only transforms your heart but also deepens your relationship with God, filling each moment with His presence and purpose.

Prayer is your lifeline to God and a pathway to victory. Embrace it, and you will discover the boundless strength and peace He provides.

Chapter 10

The Power of the Holy Spirit in Our Lives: Bearing Fruit

Imagine being lost in a dense darkness, unable to see a clear path forward. This confusion reflects the spiritual dryness many of us experience when we try to navigate life on our own. In such moments, the guidance of the Holy Spirit becomes not just helpful, but essential. The Holy Spirit brings light to our darkness, clarity to our confusion, and power to our weakness. Without His presence, our efforts are limited; with Him, we are equipped to thrive, overcome challenges, and fulfill God's purpose for our lives.

Personal Story: The Transformative Power of the Holy Spirit

During a season of spiritual dryness, I felt lost. I struggled to hear God's voice, doubting my purpose, and lacking the courage to follow God's will. Desperate, I committed to praying a monthly nine-day novena to the Infant Jesus. On the night of October 21st, during one such novena, I had a dream that profoundly changed my course.

In the dream, I sat on a platform overlooking a vast ocean. Nearby, people rested by a protective railing, gazing at the waves. Suddenly, the precious items I held slipped from my hands and teetered dangerously on the edge, about to fall into the sea. Panic gripped me, but I was too far away to reach them. Just then, a small boy appeared, calm and confident. He carefully retrieved each of my five valuable items and returned them to me.

When I awoke, the Holy Spirit revealed to me that the boy was the Infant Jesus, answering my prayer for restoration. Among the precious things restored was this very book— a project I had started over fifteen years ago but had abandoned repeatedly, doubting my ability to complete it. In that moment, I realized that this book was not just a personal idea; it was a divine calling I was now ready to embrace.

This experience taught me that my struggles were not failures but part of a refining process. I had thought I wasn't meant to write the book; instead, God was preparing me through faith and perseverance. The journey showed me the power of prayer, surrender to God's will. I also learned that true transformation and restoration come not through my effort alone but through surrendering to the Spirit's power and guidance. Thus, every accomplishment is a gift, sustained through ongoing prayer.

The Holy Spirit: Our Source of Power and Transformation

From the beginning, the Holy Spirit has been the agent of transformation. In Genesis 1:2, we read that the Spirit "hovered over the waters," bringing order out of chaos. In our lives, He works similarly, bringing clarity, healing, and strength.

Jesus Christ, knowing the essential role of the Holy Spirit, told His disciples to "stay here in the city until you have been clothed with power from on high" (Luke 24:49). This power is not only for overcoming sin and temptation but for living a life that bears lasting fruit. As Paul writes in Galatians 5:22-23, "The fruit of the Spirit is love, joy, peace, patience, kindness, generosity, faithfulness, gentleness, and self-control. There is no law against such things." These fruits are the evidence of a life guided by the Spirit.

Without the Holy Spirit, we are vulnerable to the pull of the flesh, the distractions of the world, and the enemy's schemes. But with Him, we are empowered, transformed, and able to walk in the light of Christ.

Reflection Questions
- How have you experienced the Holy Spirit's power and guidance in your life?
- In what areas do you need the Spirit's transformation and strength?

Practical Steps: Bearing Fruit through the Holy Spirit's Power

1. **Seek the Holy Spirit's Guidance Daily:** Invite the Holy Spirit into every aspect of your life: decisions, thoughts, and actions. Each morning, pray: "Holy Spirit, guide me today. Lead my thoughts, my words, and my actions according to Your will." Also, identify areas where you need transformation, whether breaking

a habit, overcoming fear, or renewing your mindset. Surrender these to the Spirit and trust His guidance.
2. **Cultivate the Fruits of the Spirit:** The fruits of the Spirit are the hallmarks of a transformed life. Focus on developing one fruit each week. For example:
    - **Week 1**: Love – Show genuine kindness to those around you.
    - **Week 2**: Patience – Practice remaining calm in challenging situations.

    Ask the Holy Spirit to nurture these fruits in you and reflect on your progress daily.
3. **Exercise Spiritual Authority Over Strongholds:** Jesus has given us authority to stand against the enemy (Luke 10:19). When facing spiritual battles, declare: "By the power of the Holy Spirit, I am free from every stronghold and curse. I claim victory in Jesus' name." This declaration of faith empowers you to overcome obstacles and resist the enemy's attacks. Remember, without faith, no one can please God
4. **Pray for Discernment and Empowerment:** The Holy Spirit equips us with discernment to recognize the enemy's schemes and with wisdom to navigate challenges and prosper in God's will.

    Pray "Holy Spirit, give me discernment to see clearly and wisdom to act rightly." This practice deepens your reliance on the Spirit and strengthens your ability to make God inspired decisions.
5. **Stay Connected to the Holy Spirit:** Maintain a strong connection with the Spirit through:

- **Daily prayer**: Consistent communication keeps you aligned with God.
- **Scripture study**: The Word reveals God's will and reinforces His promises.
- **Fellowship with believers**: Community provides support and encouragement.

These practices create fertile ground for the Holy Spirit to work powerfully in your life.

Closing Thoughts

By seeking and surrendering to the Holy Spirit daily, you open your life to transformation, freedom, and the abundant fruit Jesus promised. A Spirit-led life isn't one of striving but of thriving, rooted in God's love, empowered by His presence, and guided by His wisdom.

Chapter 11

Live in Intimacy with God: Encountering God Through Personal Experience

Moving from Knowledge About God to Truly Knowing Him

Have you ever experienced a moment so charged with God's presence that it changed you forever? Such encounters take us beyond merely knowing about God and move us to genuinely experience Him. Like Job, who declared, "I had heard of You by the hearing of the ear, but now my eye sees You; therefore, I despise myself, and repent in dust and ashes." (Job 42:5-6), we too need transformative moments to deepen our faith.

A Testimony of God's Faithfulness

I vividly recall a night that forever shaped my relationship with God. My brother and I were on a twelve-hour journey from Abuja to Port Harcourt, Nigeria. He was gravely ill, and time was against us. We needed to see a specialist urgently. Just an hour into the trip, the car broke down in the middle of nowhere.

With the help of another passenger, I carefully lifted my unconscious brother and laid him by the roadside, hoping the cool air would revive him, as he was drenched in sweat, a consequence of his condition. Meanwhile, the other passengers quickly arranged new transport and left. I was left alone with my unconscious brother, insufficient money, and no means of communication.

Desperation set in. I recalled the doctor's words just hours earlier: "What your brother needs is an ENT specialist. We don't have one in Abuja yet, and I can only pray it's not too late for him." He had prescribed six-hourly injections but warned that time was running out.

As the sounds of people boarding other vehicles faded into the night, the silence grew heavy. I prayed quietly: "My God, You know why we're traveling at night. I don't have enough money for another fare. As things stand, we may be here until morning, and by then, it may be too late for my brother.

It was a simple, heartfelt plea. Then, something extraordinary happened. A stranger from the bus approached and asked why we hadn't left. After I explained our situation, he walked away, but soon returned, almost as if compelled by an unseen force. Without hesitation, he paid our fare, a significant sum, so we could continue the journey.

That night, I encountered God, not through thunderous signs, but through the quiet prompting that moved a stranger to act. In my deepest need, God showed me His faithfulness. Today, my brother is healthy and thriving. That night's experience remains etched in my heart as a reminder that God is always present, even in our darkest hours.

Building a Deep, Personal Relationship with God

God longs for each of us to know Him and experience His love. Every joy, challenge, and moment of need is an opportunity to know Him more intimately. As we draw closer to Him, our faith matures, and our trust deepens, even in difficult circumstances.

The Journey from Distance to Intimacy

Too often, we approach God from a distance, relying on second-hand knowledge or routine prayers. True intimacy with God develops when we seek Him earnestly, engage with Him, and recognize His presence in our everyday lives.

Reflection Questions
- Recall a moment when you felt closest to God. What happened before and after that encounter?
- How can you cultivate more moments of closeness with God in your daily life?

Practical Steps to Deepen Your Relationship with God
1. **Pursue Personal Encounters with God**
   - Actively seek God in your daily experiences, and recognizing His active presence in nature, conversations, or challenges.
   - Be attentive to the subtle ways He speaks, whether through Scripture, a timely word, or a moment of peace in chaos.
   - Practice "God-awareness" throughout your day, reminding yourself that He is with you.
2. **Cultivate a Lifestyle of Gratitude**
   - A grateful heart recognizes God's presence in both blessings and challenges.

- Reflect on St. Thérèse of Lisieux's wisdom: "Everything is a grace." Even difficulties can open doors to opportunities and blessings, drawing us closer to God.
- Keep a gratitude journal to document God's goodness and faithfulness in your life.

3. **Pray with Honesty and Vulnerability**
   - Speak to God from your heart. Share your fears, struggles, and joys openly with Him.
   - Invite Him into your pain and uncertainties. Vulnerable prayers build deeper intimacy.
   - Trust that God welcomes your honesty and responds with love and grace.

4. **Reflect on God's Presence Daily**
   - End each day with a brief reflection on where you sensed God's presence.
   - Ask yourself: "How did God guide, protect, or comfort me today?" This habit shifts your perspective and fosters a deeper sense of connection with Him.
   - Immerse Yourself in Scripture: God's Word reveals His character and heart. Spend time daily reading and meditating on Scripture.
   - Pray through verses that speak to your current situation, allowing them to strengthen and guide you.

Final Words: Living for Eternity, A Life Well-Lived for God

The journey to heaven requires a heart rooted in dedication, a spirit strengthened by faith, and a life marked by perseverance. It calls us to seek God's kingdom above all else, to live with a deep understanding of who He is, and to fix our eyes firmly on eternity. God has equipped us with essential tools: His Word, laws, ordinances, repentance, prayer, and obedience to guide our steps along this path. By relying on these gifts, we can be confident that our journey is leading us ever closer to eternal life with Him.

In the end, our time on earth is fleeting, but our true destination lies in eternity with God. Every trial we endure, every act of faith, and every choice to obey shapes a life worthy of heaven's reward. Without Jesus, redemption would be impossible, but through His sacrifice, we are saved and made new.

As St. Paul encourages us, "Let us hold unswervingly to the hope we profess, for He who promised is faithful" (Hebrews 10:23). Let God's Word be your foundation, live humbly in His presence, and trust deeply in His divine plan.

This book is not just a guide: it is a call to action, a reminder that heaven is not a distant dream but a promise we are called to pursue with every fiber of our being. The path may be narrow, and the challenges daunting, but with God's grace, a heart rooted in faith, and a life committed to His will, the reward of eternal glory is within our reach.

Making heaven is about living each day with purpose, love, and an unshakable trust in God. It is in the quiet moments of prayer, the trials that refine us, and the small, consistent acts of obedience that we find our steps aligned with His.

As you close this book, I pray that you open your heart wider to God's infinite love and mercy. Let the truths and practical steps within these pages guide your journey. Remember, the victory is already ours in Christ. Hold fast to Him and press on with unwavering hope. Heaven is worth every sacrifice and every step of faith.

May the Lord bless you, strengthen you, and guide you on this holy journey. See you in heaven.

With love and prayers,
Uju Oramah

Bibliography

1. The Holy Bible. *New Revised Standard Version Catholic Edition* (NRSVCE).
2. Teresa of Ávila. *The Interior Castle.* Translated by E. Allison Peers. New York: Dover Publications, 2007. Originally published in 1577.
3. Liguori, St. Alphonsus. *Uniformity with God's Will.* Translated by Thomas W. Tobin. Rockford, IL: TAN Books, 1998.
4. St. John of the Cross. *Dark Night of the Soul.* Translated by E. Allison Peers. New York: Image Books, 1959.
5. St. Thérèse of Lisieux. *The Story of a Soul: The Autobiography of St. Thérèse of Lisieux.* Washington, DC: ICS Publications, 1996.
6. Catherine of Siena. *The Dialogue of the Seraphic Virgin Catherine of Siena.* Translated by Algar Thorold. New York: TAN Books, 1991. Originally published in 1378.
7. Thomas à Kempis. *The Imitation of Christ.* Translated by William Creighton. Mineola, NY: Dover Publications, 2003.
8. Kowalska, Maria Faustina. *Diary of Saint Maria Faustina Kowalska: Divine Mercy in My Soul.* Translated by M. Byrnes. 3rd ed. Stockbridge, MA: Marian Press, 2005.
9. Mother Teresa. *Come Be My Light: The Private Writings of the Saint of Calcutta.* Edited by Brian Kolodiejchuk. New York: Doubleday, 2007.

♥ Thank You for Your Support!

👉 Get your free workbook for **ABC of Making Heaven** at ujuoramah.com.

👉 We'd love to hear your thoughts! Share your reviews on Amazon, Twitter, and Goodreads.

Need help writing or publishing your book? We can assist you—no prior experience needed! Visit divinechildpublishers.com or email us at divinechildpublishers@gmail.com.

For hard copies, bulk orders, new releases, and updates, email

✉ divinechildpublishers@gmail.com.

or visit:

👉 divinechildpublishers.com

👉 ujuoramah.com

For author interviews, speaking engagements, or more information, email us at:

✉ divinechildpublishers@gmail.com.

MOTIVATE and INSPIRE OTHERS!
"Share This Book"

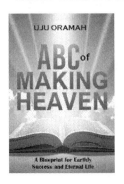

Retail 10.99
Special Quantity Discount
Plus, Shipping

5-9 Books	6.99
10-20 Books	5.99
21-99	4.99
100-499	3.99
500+	3.50

Order and let us know if you want us to help you share it for free with those who need it. Thank you, and may God bless you richly in Jesus's Name.

To Place Order-Email:<u>divinechildpublishers@gmail.com</u>

ENGAGE MRS. UJU ORAMAH AS THE IDEAL PROFESSIONAL SPEAKER FOR YOUR NEXT FAITH EVENT

Organizations seeking to develop and strengthen the faith of their members, whether adults or teenagers, can benefit from her keynote speeches or workshop training. She will ignite passion, deepen faith, and inspire your audience.

TO CONTACT OR BOOK:

Mrs. Uju Oramah
Email: divinechildpublishers@gmail.com

SOME OTHER BOOKS BY THE AUTHOR
Get your copies from **Amazon.com.**

1. **St. Padre Pio's 36-Week Spiritual Journey** – Deepen your faith with this transformative devotional inspired by St. Padre Pio. Includes St. Pio's powerful healing prayers to guide you toward spiritual growth.
2. **Meditative Thoughts for Empowerment: 30 Days of Spiritual Reflection and Renewal** – This inspiring book offers a heartfelt blend of personal stories, scripture insights, and practical wisdom to help you find peace, strength, and renewal.
3. **Igbo Picture Book for Kids and Beginners** – Make learning Igbo fun and engaging with this vibrant bilingual picture book! Perfect for kids and beginners.
4. **Mastering Igbo Language: A Comprehensive Guide for Beginners, Intermediate, and Advanced Learners** – More than just a guide, this book immerses you in the heart of the Igbo language.
5. **Billy the Smart Turtle and the Cruel Lioness:** A ruthless lioness preyed on the kingdom's young. When Billy's turn came, his mother sent him. Would he outwit the lioness?
6. **Thorns and Roses** – A poetic glimpse into the journey of life, capturing both its beauty and challenges through heartfelt stories and reflections.

DISCOVER DEEPER FAITH AND IGBO LANGUAGE MASTERY WITH UJU ORAMAH ✝

As a dedicated Christian author, Uju crafts books and blogs that deepen your connection with God. Master the Igbo language with her comprehensive guides, and be uplifted by her inspiring storybooks. Discover a transformative way to experience God's presence today!

Christian Books ### Children's Story Book

Audio Books     **Music Mp4**

Igbo Language

 Igbo Picture Book for Kids and Beginners

Poems

 Laminated Posters in English & Igbo. Size-16.5x23 inches

Uju Oramah

Made in the USA
Columbia, SC
17 March 2025

55281040R00041